POCAHONTAS

Girl of Jamestown

by Kate Jassem
illustrated by Allan Eitzen

Troll Associates

Troll Associates,
Library of Congress Catalog Card Number: 78-18045
ISBN 0-89375-142-1

10 9 8 7 6 5 4 3

POCAHONTAS

Girl of Jamestown

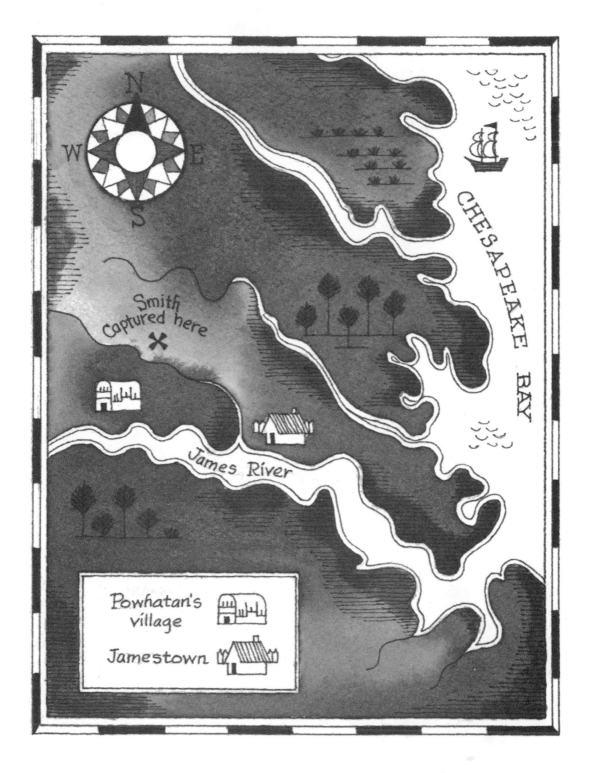

The Indian boy knew he was being followed. He moved faster. The dry leaves rustled behind him. Suddenly, he stopped. He listened. A twig snapped!

Quickly, he turned and took aim with his bow and arrow.

"Stop!" Pocahontas cried out. "Don't shoot me, Nantequas!"

"So, little sister, you have followed me again!"

"Nantequas, you must come home. They have caught one of the white men! They are bringing him to our father tonight!"

Nantequas began to run.

Pocahontas laughed as the wind blew through her long black hair.

They raced toward the village of their father, Chief Powhatan.

The village was noisy with excitement. Pocahontas knew there would be a big feast.

All summer and fall she had heard about the strangers who had come to her father's land. She had wanted to see these strangers with her own eyes. Now at last she would have her wish.

Smoke rose from the bark-covered wigwams that circled the village. In the clearing, turkeys and deer were already roasting on open fires.

That night, Powhatan, mighty Chief of more than thirty Algonkian tribes, sat on his throne of mats in the longhouse.

He looked splendid to Pocahontas. He was dressed in a coonskin robe, and his face was painted in many colors. He wore bright feathers and beads. Behind him stood his tall sons and his best warriors.

But Pocahontas had never seen Powhatan look so troubled.

9

The white men had come in three tall ships in the spring. They had sailed far up into the bay of the Great Water.

When they began to build their huts, some of Chief Powhatan's tribes had fought them. But others had been friendly. They had traded corn for the settlers' beads.

Powhatan felt the danger that might come from these people. They had fire-sticks that thundered and killed. They were on Indian lands.

Now one of their leaders had been brought here by the Pamunkey tribe. This man said he was looking for the Great Chief Powhatan.

Two warriors held the prisoner. His feet and hands were tied. They pushed him, and he fell near the blazing fire.

Loud shouting filled the longhouse.

"Silence!" commanded Powhatan.

He turned to the prisoner.

"You are called John Smith?"

The man nodded.

"Untie his hands. First we will eat. Then we will talk."

10

Pocahontas could not eat. Her father's men seemed angry. Some of the children screamed when the white man looked their way.

But Pocahontas looked at his blue eyes and wondered why they feared him.

"He looks like a friend," she thought.

After the feast, Powhatan spoke.

"You, Smith, are Chief of the white men who come to my land?"

"No, mighty Powhatan. My leader lives across the Great Water. He is King James of England. He sent us to this land."

Powhatan answered in anger.

"I am King here! This is my land! We have watched you hunt with loud fire-sticks and chop trees from our woods. We have waited for you to leave as other white men have done. But now you build houses. You plant crops on Indian land."

"Mighty Chief, there is much land. My people come in peace to trade with you."

Smith took beads from his coat, but Powhatan turned away.

Pocahontas trembled with fear. What would her father do?

The Chief raised his hand.

"John Smith, you must die!"

13

Two warriors threw Smith to the ground. Now the strongest warrior raised a heavy stone club.

In one blow, the white man would be dead.

"No!" Pocahontas screamed.

She ran to the prisoner and threw herself over him.

"Please, Father, give him to me!"

The warrior put down his club. The prisoner's life would be spared.

It was a law among Powhatan's people that a woman of the tribe could save a prisoner with these words.

Powhatan looked at Pocahontas. Why had she done this?

"Perhaps she is right," he thought. "If we kill Smith, his men might come with their fire-sticks. Maybe it is better to let him live."

A few days later, Powhatan's tribe adopted Captain Smith. They called him Nantaquoud.

"You were spared because I asked it," said Pocahontas. "Now you become one of us. It is our way."

For many days Captain Smith stayed in the Indian village. Pocahontas hoped he would never leave.

He told them more about his King and his home across the sea. Powhatan listened. He wanted peace for his people. But he did not like the settlers. There would be trouble.

Finally, Powhatan named twelve braves to lead Captain Smith back to his people in Jamestown.

"Do not go," Pocahontas begged.

John Smith smiled at his friend. "I will come again soon, little Princess."

When the braves returned from Jamestown, they told of the sickness among Captain Smith's people.

"They have little to eat," they said. "They do not know how to find food. Already many have died."

18

Powhatan thought, "Now perhaps they will go back across the sea and leave us alone."

But Pocahontas felt pain in her heart for her friend.

"Father," she said, "John Smith is now our brother. We cannot let his people starve. We must help them."

All during that winter and spring, Pocahontas brought food to the Jamestown settlers. They grew very fond of her. She had saved their lives.

The Indian Princess was generous and kind, yet she was also full of fun. Her nickname, Pocahontas, meant "Playful One."

The Indians told Powhatan of the shiny tools and weapons they saw in the fort.

"If I can trade our corn and game for fire-sticks and hatchets," Powhatan thought, "we will have much power from these white men."

Captain Smith sent Powhatan many presents in return for the food Pocahontas was bringing. He sent bells, mirrors, bright copper, and beads.

But he did not send guns.

Powhatan was not pleased.

Late in 1608, another boat came from England, carrying gifts for the Chief.

The English King had been told of Powhatan's great tribes. He wanted to make friends with this powerful leader. This would mean good trading for the settlers at Jamestown. He knew they must have the Indians' help to survive.

Now Captain Smith brought Powhatan a huge bed, a beautiful red silk cape, and a copper crown.

But Powhatan refused to kneel to have the crown placed on his head.

"Powhatan bows to no one!" he said.

Captain Smith had to stand on his toes to put the crown on the tall Chief's head!

More and more settlers were coming to Jamestown. The Indians were restless. Some wanted to kill all these strangers who were living on sacred lands. Many began to steal tools and guns. The colonists were frightened. But they had a hard winter to face, and they needed food.

Captain Smith decided to visit the Great Chief again.

"No more!" said Powhatan. "We have given you much corn. But you have given us toys. Take your people and go. You must leave the Indians' land."

The warriors moved closer to the white men. Pocahontas was afraid for her friends.

But Captain Smith pulled out his pistol. His men lifted their muskets. "You will give us corn, Powhatan!"

The Chief was terribly angry. But he knew that bows and arrows were no match for guns.

"I will give you food. But I will not forget this!"

23

Soon afterward, Pocahontas heard her father talking to his men in low whispers.

"Before the sunrise, the Englishmen must die."

"We will do it now!"

"No!" Powhatan commanded. "We will wait until they sleep. I have sent food for their fire. Let them think it is a sign of peace."

Pocahontas knew what she had to do. Soon it would be dark. She had no time to waste.

24

Her heart pounded as she ran through the woods to Captain Smith.

"You must go at once!" she cried. "My father's men are coming to kill you tonight!"

"Once again you have saved my life, my little Princess."

Tears streamed down her cheeks as she went back to her father's longhouse.

The troubles between the English and the Indians became worse. People on both sides were wounded. A few were killed, and some were captured.

As the anger grew in Powhatan's heart, Captain Smith became more determined. He would not fail the settlers at Jamestown!

He put the people to work building a big blockhouse. They dug a freshwater well inside the fort. A new roof was put on the church, and more houses were built.

Captain Smith sent many colonists outside the fort walls that spring and summer to dig and plant fields. They were helped by friendly Indians.

But while the Englishmen were learning the Indian ways of planting and hunting, the Indians were learning more and more about the white man's ways of fighting—with swords and guns!

And an old friend was not among them to help any more. Powhatan had forbidden Pocahontas ever to visit Jamestown again.

More ships came.

Then one day word came that Captain Smith was gone!

"He will not live to reach England," an Indian spy told Powhatan and Pocahontas. "Powder from the fire-sticks exploded. He was almost dead when they carried him to the boat!"

"Good!" said Powhatan. "Now they are without their leader. Maybe now they will go away."

Pocahontas cried until she could cry no more.

Powhatan led his people deeper and deeper into the forest. He wanted to drive the English out of his land forever, but how could he fight without guns?

"Here we will find more game to hunt. Here we will be safe from their fire-sticks," he told his

people. "We will let the English starve without our corn."

From the forest he sent warriors to spy and steal guns. They did not always come back.

The Jamestown settlers called that winter the "Starving Time." They did not have Pocahontas to bring them food and laughter. They did not have Captain Smith to make them work hard.

When John Smith had left in August, there were five hundred people in Jamestown. By the end of the winter, only about sixty people were still living!

In May of 1610, two small boats sailed up the river toward the fort. Their passengers had been shipwrecked the summer before in Bermuda on the way to Jamestown.

Now, instead of finding a busy, growing settlement, they found many empty houses and a great stillness. Sick and discouraged, the remaining colonists had lost hope.

On June 7, the leaders gave orders to abandon Jamestown.

But just as they were setting sail, a large ship came into view. It was loaded with food, supplies, and new settlers from England!

Many cried with relief as they held a service of thanksgiving in their small church.

Maybe Jamestown would survive after all.

Every year, more and more colonists came. Powhatan's heart grew heavy as he realized that the English meant to stay in his land forever.

They brought seeds and tools and supplies from England. They brought strange birds that did not fly, and squealing hogs that grew fat for roasting. They built more pointed houses, and planted great fields of corn and beans.

They made the fort stronger. Smoke rose from the chimneys of new houses.

Craftsmen and carpenters came to live in Jamestown. The people made tar and pitch. They made glass, and wood ashes for soap. They chopped down trees and split the wood to make clapboard. They collected sassafras roots for medicine. They hoped to send these things back to England to sell.

But the fighting and killing continued between the Indians and the settlers.

And Pocahontas was not seen anywhere.

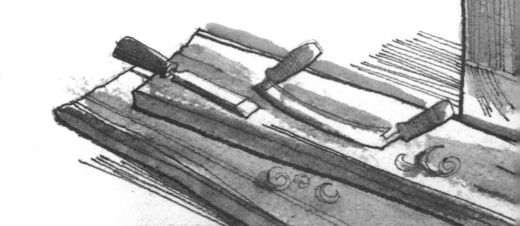

In December, 1613, Captain Samuel Argall sailed from the fort at Jamestown to a friendly Indian village far up the Potomac River. He wanted to find corn and game there, since Powhatan would not let the Indians near Jamestown trade with the settlers.

He was also there because he had heard that Pocahontas was visiting this tribe.

The village Chief welcomed Captain Argall.

"We come in peace to trade," the Captain said. His men brought cloth, beads, pots and pans from the ship.

"How beautiful!" the Chief's wife exclaimed as she held a copper kettle in her hands. "Look, Pocahontas!"

Captain Argall turned. He looked at the young woman.

"You are Pocahontas, daughter of Chief Powhatan?"

Pocahontas nodded and stepped back. She did not like the look in the Englishman's eyes.

The Captain and the Chief talked together for a long time.

By sunset, the Chief had traded Pocahontas for a copper kettle! She would be taken back to Jamestown as a hostage.

The colonists hoped that Powhatan would send back all the prisoners he had captured and all the guns he had taken, in return for Pocahontas.

The Chief did not want any harm to come to his daughter. But he knew that the English had always been her friends.

He sent back many prisoners and promised friendship and corn, but he did not send back the guns.

As the months passed, Pocahontas tried to find peace in her heart. The colonists were kind to her. She was free to visit from house to house. She had a warm room, pretty clothes, and food to eat. The people loved her.

By spring, the Indian Princess had many new friends. One of them was John Rolfe. It was not long before they had fallen in love.

In April, he asked her to be his wife.

Powhatan would not come to Jamestown for his daughter's wedding. The proud Chief had vowed never to set foot on English territory. But he sent his brother and two of his sons.

In a church filled with flowers, Pocahontas took the English name of Rebecca, and married John Rolfe.

All of Jamestown was there.

The marriage in 1614 of the young Jamestown leader and the beautiful Indian Princess brought great joy to the people. And it also brought a long period of better feelings between the Indians and the colonists.

For the next eight years, people spoke of the "Peace of Pocahontas."

Pocahontas and John were very happy. He took her to his farm in the new town of Henrico, near Jamestown. Here they planted fields of corn, beans, and tobacco.

When spring came again, they had a baby boy, Thomas.

Their English friends came from Jamestown to see the baby. Powhatan let some of Pocahontas' sisters and brothers visit, too.

In 1613, John had sent the first shipload of his tobacco to the Old World. The Indians had smoked tobacco for many years, but their tobacco was harsh and bitter. Rolfe invented new ways of planting and curing tobacco from the West Indies. It was not long before this tobacco became the colony's most important crop.

In 1616, the leaders in Jamestown decided to send Pocahontas and John Rolfe to England. They wanted to convince King James that the sale of tobacco would make a lot of money for England.

They were also proud of their Indian Princess.

John was happy and excited. "I want to show you so many beautiful things in London," he told Pocahontas.

They set sail for England in the very same boat in which Captain Argall had brought Pocahontas to Jamestown in 1613!

After many long weeks at sea, they reached London. Pocahontas could not believe her eyes! She had never before seen so many people and so many houses . . . and there was so much noise!

Many feasts and great balls were given in honor of Pocahontas. The people were fascinated by her. They followed her about as she was taken to see the sights of London.

Before long, a message came from Queen Anne. She wanted to meet the Princess who had saved the lives of so many Englishmen.

44

Pocahontas delighted everyone who met her. But she thought often of her homeland across the sea. She missed the open spaces, the clear blue sky, the fresh-smelling air.

One day a visitor was announced. When Pocahontas came into the room, she found herself once again looking into the blue eyes of John Smith!

"But they did tell me you were dead!" she cried. "Why did you not tell me you were still alive?"

She covered her face with her hands and ran from the room. It was hours before she could talk to her old friend.

As the days in London grew cold and damp, Pocahontas began to feel weary. There was much sickness in England. The Indians who had made the journey with her became ill. Soon two of them died.

The fog made everyone uneasy. There was no sunshine. Now Thomas was sick, too. Pocahontas wondered if she would ever see her home again.

In March, 1617, they set sail down the Thames River toward the sea.

But Pocahontas did not even live long enough to see the Great Water again. She became so sick that the boat had to dock, and John Rolfe carried her to shore at Gravesend, England.

47

Pocahontas was only about 22 years old when she died, far away from her home. John Rolfe sadly returned to Jamestown.

The people who had known the Indian Princess grieved. Pocahontas had done much for Jamestown. It was her help that enabled the struggling colony, the first permanent settlement in America, to survive.

It was Pocahontas who planted the seeds of friendship that linked the Old World with the New World.

And it was the son of Pocahontas and John Rolfe who was the first of many generations of Virginians in the proud new country of America.